Halfway Friends for Decades

Halfway Friends for Decades

Poems by Elizabeth Carmer

Word Poetry

Published by Word Poetry
P.O. Box 541106
Cincinnati, OH 45254-1106

ISBN: 9781625493231

Poetry Editor: Kevin Walzer
Business Editor: Lori Jareo

Cover photo: Elizabeth Carmer

Visit us on the web at www.wordpoetrybooks.com

Table of Contents

Maintain Belief

Women can do this, too.
Their own ruling is intentional.
Religion allegedly supports a land.

The sinking of land is that women are to be treated first.
The historical marking of man-versus-man has led to graves.
A graveyard is a location to walk, stand or kneel.

Men typically cultivated the dirt.
And women joined the procession.
A gravesite is an example of good land.

It's up to the reader to decide what the capture of land means.
As a fire exposes the surrounding air,
A flame captures scenes of a crime.

A photograph documents territory and can be
influential, like knowing that a memoir does not
recount the price of a flag but insinuates feeling.

Some say bribery goes hand in hand with gain,

but countless counteract given biblical references.

Like that two men, Cain and Abel, shared a Father.

Murder occurs at sea in order to eliminate evidence.

Intelligence is often so remote, the aftermath of death is undefined.

A presidential nation is sought by the heartfelt.

Sinking has nothing to do with physical incapacitation.

Sinking is espionage which was ruined.

The counter effect of the truth is medicinal.

Treatment and trauma maintain speed at which women can see.

The sinking of land is invisible but its presence is shown through
  the effects of prejudices.

A presidential funeral is a must-see and firearm is a conjugated verb.

The Silhouette

The woman Eva Peron was the wife
of a president. She attempted to settle inequity.
Illustrating an immaculate performance,
like Madonna. Like the government,
she had a motive. Like a woman in a nation,
she had to be talkative. A woman

in a Hispanic society appears
to be an actress. The relation between Evita
and America is through cinema.
The time of Evita knew a class conflict.
Argentina was historically indigenous, the opposite
of a war caught on tape. As Madonna, real

actress, shed light on Evita, her personification
of the Argentinian conflict overshadowed
the conception of opposition. Doubt
about Evita still exists today, as her cancer
was traumatic, and so too was the social divide.
Talking to the proletariat is not hardship.

Distance is the essence of confusion.
Talk among nations can either create
or dispel fear. A female voice
contributes to foreign solidarity. The
echo of fame excludes personal ambition,
and then familiarity becomes widespread.

Excusing bourgeoisie is not a crime.
From poor to rich the proximity of not
knowing between the people creates a
nation. The birth of truth is not the death
of a nation. Madonna portrayed a rising voice
accepting fame. We, as Americans,

can see that culminating persona
not abandoning her role
and declaring welfare of the state
an absolute. We can see the silhouette of a woman
being applied to history nationally,
however short the period of time.

Made to be a Movie, 1950s

The highlight of life is not read nor spoken
it's with whom you meet; we wonder
if everyone has one. It is wanting to see
what mingling is and all of the in-between.
The movies, the glam and then the shame

of "Who said that?" Or, not lying about
being female and asking who hunted that.
She is us, a president's wife. California
talk was adjacent to nothing. Its bottomless
void sought out the future. Cuba was deemed

a bright nation. A lone star student in Florida
may decide to take on medicine and attempt
to encounter a foreign epidemic. The bright
thought of being inside an office building made
us build up and wait to see what becomes

of it. The unmotivated news to fear the worst
which could have cost a life. The theory
behind space exploration means invading
Russia. Literacy became a social event like
the age race and racial market. The draft

could be confusing and draw back fear from
centuries ago, but serving is prudent for some.
Vernacular was important as well as social
graces. The practice of grace before dinner
began to replace the act of churchgoing.

Homelessness evaded the Cold War and streets
became more systematic. The nonsensical idea
that pools were flattery was almost like saying
Barbie was unpopular. Tried and true, vernacular
sprung in the kitchen with its modernizing façade.

The Unspoken Catalan

The arrival of the bull in Barcelona does not
change the state. In the same moment, Madrid
feels shame but Barcelona located itself next
to the sea to avoid that devastation. Madrid can
feel the stress as a priest can when no one

attends mass. The cup of wine is like powder
of a war. Catholicism is a crux for people to
think what others are thinking. The Rock of
Gibraltar is a focal point and the straight
separates Spain and Morocco. The queen

marries the people. And France alone holds
the power in the Basque country, which
Franco knew already. One cannot ignore
the mule that could have constructed Spain.
The time and distance from Madrid to Barcelona

is only a tourist seeing a wind turbine. The dust
in the corner of a church is the manner of a nation.
Like a flamenco dancer's toe touching the floor
in Sevilla, the harrowing embarrassment of women
recalling when they have worn heels. The shock and

horror of the blood on the torero, or bullfighter. It's a
gilded nation with its architecture and cathedrals.
The name Gaudi resonates only to some, and those
educated in fine arts. But Gaudi architecture never
left Spain and so its name is provisional. La Rambla

resembles nothing of flamenco. There is spit on
the street from the gypsies. Gypsy women do
curtail the tourists and average Spaniard. By their
wandering around asking for money. If they know
the current market value and name of Spanish

currency, we feel threat. Their commerce is not
terrorism but stealing and theft. They wandered
here aware of the warnings and the overall
public dissatisfaction. They don't know the royal
family nor have they seen them. People don't

lose sleep that gypsies are endangered and could
be man-handled during a street cleaning. Gypsies
cannot hear the muezzin's prayer occurring in
Morocco, even if from there and its memory rings
in their heads. Their turbans are self-defense.

God Speed

A favor is not a handshake and people forget
Brazilians speak Portuguese. It's a country
to know, given its rising population. We know

men are not the enemy here. Human guilt
is not their art scene. Surpassing the age
of seventeen is not criminal. Women of all

ages go to the beach. The favela in Brazil is
different than the morro, like the difference
between running and escaping. Drug trade

in Rio, does it involve tourists? We cannot know.
There are tourists and there are volunteers. They
pay with deposits to banks, so they are the bad

people, in broken English. Like how baile funk
differs outside Rio and inside of Rio. The baile
funk translates as a strong rhythm. Turning an

individual to dance towards a reckless fire.
Its flame sheds light and creates a spirit of
origin, to hide lingering shame in a favela.

Ipanema beach is crowded and Carnival occupies
the streets. Public health is a voice lost and unknown,
like the Amazon and its track. The acai is the color

of muddled red. The guarana is a flavor known.
The Brazilian police on and off occupy the streets.
The heat is an excuse for everything in general.

Halfway Friends for Decades

So Lindsey was visiting from, oh where was it, oh, one step richer than New Canaan, CT. She was visiting me in Spanish Harlem. We know each other from either sports (across town), tanning or babysitting in upstate NY. Both of us went to college, separately, and met each other from third grade. Lindsey decided, as she did, to tan (kind of), shop and commit slander. I was working full time at Anthropologie in SoHo. Still very much Manhattan these days, even to New Yorkers and travelers. I lived in a two-bedroom apartment, with the lightbulb dim and not replaced, maybe due to retail work scheduling. I became inured to subway transportation, not a hard route to take but circumstantial and convenient. I guess Lindsey wanted to make a splash coming in because she worked at Splash in Greenwich, CT. But she didn't make "an entrance" because I felt uncomfortable with slander. Lindsey's parents were executives and therefore the term pj's could be slang in America. Lindsey began in high school to use a fake ID and carried the same one to college. She brought that ID to NYC while visiting me, which got us into a club in lower Manhattan, where neither of us had been before. Did our friendship end that day? No, it just became remote.

Burning Grasses

Of Vietnam's sea, is the salt as salty as the Dead
Sea? People must notice the difference, if and only
if the act of floating was internationally acceptable.

Towards the coast is an epiphany for most. The daily
encounter with ocean waves is somehow glorious but
ultimately resistant. Travel is mainly true, not hard.

Encountering the Devil is unbeknownst to most people
and inhabitants of dry land. Such as when the Devil
decides to become invincible and acts on behalf.

Or when the Devil throws a planet, named Sun,
a flame. He intends to overshadow the night by
borrowing souls to tell a story of a God. Planet

Mercury is visible and soundproof, not similar to
the meaning of Buddhism. To witness an act can
allow personal defamation of good and evil.

The fort of earth is human kindness. Solitude is dry heaving while desire is only nutrients. Solidarity is only anticipation which is actually fire made by you.

And confusion is only a made-up phenomenon. Not a mandate to destroy nor steal but an approach to an intervention that foreshadows belief or betrayal.

Newton for a Day

A job is an atom of a duty. The script to do
is constructed day by day. An element of
success is indicative of rule setting. Science
determines all else, then God determines

just human behavior. Ions are electricity in
a house. Planets culminate to eliminate fear.
Reading is a matter of fact. Glasses are an
example of the means to make it happen.

Astrology cries wind at all costs. The general
eye sees insult. The curvature of wind creates
new life form. A tree is planted to become tall
one day. Seeing green is retrospective. Seeing

blue is temperamental. National standards of
understanding are presidential, like the human
capacity to breathe. Seeing a rainbow is a true
determinant science exists in the civilian life.

A Broken Art Form

What is a successful cremation?
A fake shrine can only implode
and spark either threat or the memory

of threat. The residual effects of a fake
shrine manipulate that death is a theme;
everything then becomes a story

and we imagine a broken horizon.
People see a victim as good and not
bad. Its soul then reappears looking

to be a witness. We see rain, we see
smoke and we see fire. A human
relapses into retreat when alive

and identifies a religion, to create.
The fallen ash is not a name nor
a grave; it is a realization that we

cannot break the sound barrier.
The void an echo creates describes
a soul. An awakening when seeking

nirvana is perception alone. A soul
pierces the human, not a god. Karma
evolves from trials and tribulations.

A wound is a gut instinct to act, sky
is a humane distance from earth
and personification remains alive.

The Tree

During a storm
you hear

a branch crack
and wonder

if that will fall
on your house.

Just then
is fear an option?

Like a Shadow

is an existence, a cave hides
daylight. It even hides shadows
and therefore personality.

Perspiration is not about falling,
it's progress of paranoia. A soul
can escape during an awakening

of fear. The person contends
the world below. Anguish, solitude
make one think of a ghost. A person

loses awareness of feeling. A person
responds to noise and seeks immediate
destiny. They begin to renounce heaven

as hell and then think they hear or see
a ghost. To catch a glimpse of a ghost
is fleeting. A person then feels remorse

like they are awaiting purgatory. The ghost
may have passed through them or wind
in the cave created a lasting illusion.

The Dark Coast of Africa

A biblical truth is the aridness
of Israel. Not understanding
is trying to explain nearly nothing.

The vividness of the northern coast
of Africa is not a physical norm. Texts
reference dark appearances. Waves

crashing do not reach the highest
levels, which is not yet land. The
rocks include jagged and uneven

footing. The coast is not intended
to be walked upon but barges carry
visitors and dock at the approachable

entrance. The arrival to Africa is truly
a language barrier. People seldom do
speak Arabic and randomly attempt

to speak French. The mood is unknown
to travelers as men in baggy clothing
sleep on sidewalks without intervention.

The entrance into a bazaar is the idea
that seeing is believing. A guided tour
can only allow one to perceive what

is actually education. To appear to know
is not a drawback nor an illegal stance.
Men and women comingle but in different

clothing. Non-western values and people
instill their traditional daily ritual while
foreigners can only fear their footing.

High School Civility

This was a high school sorority and not a college sorority. So the definition of sister lost its meaning. Per the rules and set guidelines of this sorority, there were held meetings; one on a Sunday evening was at the house of the president. Each upper member had to choose their own youngest sister, to one day escort to a field party. The president chose the sophomore with her same name, Jessica, a girl who pretended to be an upperclassman. One particular Sunday evening meeting, the girls, and only girls, would come to the house through the front door. As they all intended to be just, they all took their shoes off and left them on the front rug. The mom who lived there took pictures of all forty pairs of shoes. The girl Jessica who thought she could pretend to be the president blurted out, "I'm stalked." The long lasting concern of this outburst has proven atypical. The pretender Jessica has relied on a falsified hierarchy. She failed at understanding what all girls meant and she later became Prom Queen.

When a Deer Sees a Coyote

The woods was behind the house.
You can see into the house from outside.
The first floor of the house is always
with electricity on. The woods is quiet

but there are animals at night. A person
inside the house saw a coyote walking
through the woods. One of the legs
of the coyote was injured. At the time

of the spotting, the coyote was not
hungry, only walking. To cross
a trail in a woods is to seek out a deer.
A doe can never be seen nor heard.

They travel at a jot. Their eyes jolt when
approaching a trail, trees look dark, bark
looks nude and deer see the naked eye.

What is Triage?

Is it the courage to fight an epidemic? Is it a statistical approach like psychiatric epidemiology? We have modern-day catastrophes that require manpower to fix. To fix is subliminal

and not a race. Time is important during a national event or a national emergency. Spectators

mingle or watch and we understand the act of watching as historical and allowed. We are not caught

criminally when watching an event, but rather, we are people able to view. The afterthought or consequences of an event linger. When a spectator lingers, does that become criminal? Consequently, we seek out meaning. The attempt at a soliloquy is not dangerous but rather an example of what not to give. Our leaving the event is not a disappearance, that would be impossible, but an unusual amount of apprehension. Nowadays, we try to improve, either day by day or day to day. We forget what we actually like to do but remember to do something.

Upon the Reading of Her Diary

After I found out she read my diary, I made up the following: she stated this out loud: "I noticed you." That three-word statement was so open-ended that I could pretend it happened. I started to not think in sounds nor walk due to palpable fear. My feelings were so distant that I began to walk quietly. I also had a constant relationship with self. Always fearing the worst but imagining the best. I tended to oscillate between good and bad. The concept and dutiful seeking of "best in America" was made one day against me, which I also made up. I tried to become a walking ghost. I was waiting for the moment to enter the cafeteria and see people point at me. I began to listen to music and attribute it to mathematics; the technique was the memorization of radio stations. The hope of a Cinderella outcome that day slipped away and I immediately realized that I was an underachiever.

Remembering How to Wait Tables

The Southern accent is not the most desperate part
of North Carolina. The proximity to Tennessee is
not confusing. A debutante may make an appearance.

The overall geographic diversity of the state permits
an appreciation and commitment to want to visit.
The theory behind North Carolina was that it was

a centralized Southern state. But if you actually visit
towns, you may wonder how deep is the South here.
The penetration of the Deep South collides with cities.

There are mixed towns with two or more predominant
races but there are also towns made up of one race.
The census still makes it to households in that state.

There is an outside influence for the people to behave,
still use the term Yankee and call it the North. They
speak slower, handle cash and registers slower, while

also ordering slower and delivering food slower in
practically every food locale and/or coffee shop. I have
seen the old cotton industry, even if closed, in one town.

Therefore it existed and extends itself to Confederacy.
The state upholds status quo or literacy through their
collegiate undergrads and grads. A Southern belle does

also attend college. The discrepancy between Southern
charm and Southern pride is a state determination privately.
We continue to struggle with this national discrepancy.

Time Table

Time of events
is meaningless.

Time is not
good nor bad,

but simply
a cause

for the mind
to function,

the heart to rest
in mindlessness.

Robbed: A Truth of the Bible

An angel was discovered in a town one day.
The angel fell from the sky to the earth.
The path was asymmetrical like that of the stars.
But the air was translucent, hiding day and night

and whispering through the wind. Opposite
of the truth is psychological torture.
The angel crossed the bearings of servitude.
And his consciousness recognized the sun.

The town didn't care its name nor the name
of the town. The people only wanted to see
the angel. The angel remained in a garden
of a man and a woman. People traveled

to see the angel in the garden. The angel
did not speak the same language, for this
people wanted to involve the church. Money
was exchanged for viewing so a priest came.

The priest did not commit slander but he did
not think the figure was an angel. Upon view,
the angel did not change its state nor its attitude.
The man and woman could continue to accept

money but then decided to not have guests
in their house. The angel was not affected
by the laws of the town and he maintained
his personal treaty and did not convert.

Men and women continued to present to view.
The priest eventually decided that the angel
arrived as an unfortunate victim of a crime.
The angel may have been robbed by a man.

Then, by accident, the angel woke up in town.
With the awakening, the angel began to think
in reality. He, the angel, did not want to suffer
any more lapses and decided to flee the scene.

No Pity for Quijote

Don Quijote lost sanity,
despaired haphazardly,
where was his father?

Did that age wrong him,
mocking his innocence?
Or was he really just

A fool deserving laughter.
A prologue to his title
Don was the Inquisition.

Hallelujah

was once
spoken out loud.

The speaker
knew either

war was over
or gospel sung.

The Statue

The irony of Corcovado.
Its presence and stance
promote its appearance

and overshadow stigma.
Its demeanor and shadow
oversee dwellings below.

Rio offers it as panoramic
view of belief in God via
Jesus Christ, Redeemer.

A symbol of redemption
which sees national crime
as sacrificial/superficial.

To Question a Pirate

A pirate
is a pirate,
no matter
which sea.
Do they
always,
seldom
or never
have missing
teeth?

To Question a Pirate, Continued

Money is sparse
or stolen. Looted
coins are never
thrown overboard.

To walk the plank
maybe a captain
heard about mutiny

and the crew quieted.
Sailors say "Ahoy";
pirates whisper and wait
for the plank.

NYC Commuter

The monotony of a subway ride is like boring
reading. We cannot wonder out loud while
commuting, nor can we get off at the wrong
stop thinking that will help now or in the end.

Common, public travel is passed generation
to generation. A generation gap is conclusive
like the fact that NYC is situated around subway
lines. The historical nature of NYC

as an island permits people to see its relation
to the Statue of Liberty. We don't forget names
of other boroughs but we see Harlem as somehow
more distant, even when so close. Manhattan

is both large and orderly, which means
it feels no threat from Boston or Washington.
Around SoHo is a better place to shop,
Chinatown is still influential, so is the East Village,

and the Brooklyn Bridge feels like a tourist trap.
The accent is thick in the city like downtown
is tough on money. We believe that NYC must
be worth seeing even if we don't see an actor.

A Junkyard is Not Just a Place

A junkyard is like a broken switch.
To some it may be ignorance, while
others think it is an opportunity.

What you find there comes from
somewhere you will never be able
to trace. We look through rubble

and remember that these things, even
vices, are others' former belongings.
Do I want, need or love that?

Often, we forget that we actually
cannot access a junkyard. Like
not being able to access another's

backyard, to enter would be trespass.
The owner is not someone truly
familiar to us. It is a total stranger

who must have founded that place.
Others may have been involved
to give this quirky place its purpose.

Follow the Yellow Brick Road

That is an actual sidewalk painted
yellow to mimic that book by Frank
Baum. You will never see Dorothy,

Toto or the Munchkins on it, only
residents of Chittenango proper.
But maybe a renowned author

or an avid student read the book
and wants to see it. Fantasy aside,
we can determine Chittenango

as located in Upstate New York.
Where there are not tornadoes,
nor a historical event of witch

hunting or spotting. It is a town
bordering a lake with access to
many corn and onion fields. Drive

some miles and you are in Syracuse,
a city! There is a railroad crossing
state lines, too. Frank Baum, born

in the Village of Chittenango, wrote
that wonderful book. His adversary
is not the landscape of that locale.

Even remote, there are options. Not,
too many mills or factories but there
must be a means to make a living.

Commerce is not only the Erie Canal.
Sylvan Beach, down the road, offers
only what you can imagine, rides.

The Purpose of Reading

Do we feel compatible with society when we relate through reading?

We begin to think in heroic possibility

because we all think in the now and want to begin to anticipate

   something more.

The question fueling this debate is what is a hero?

On the overall conceptual hierarchy, we seek out mourning.

We can hear on the news that someone helped another.

Is loss always controversial or are we too influenced just then?

We turn to thought, not prayer and hope that we caught on to the plot.

My mistake was that I could not remember every character name. I try

to imply that doesn't happen in my personal life, which is allegedly

   without problems.

The hero must be the one whose name is repeated the most.

We actually can personally attest, but not testify, that subliminally we

   know

that the books we read do not source their own TV show.

We know that genre titles are actual etymology, a word we search the

   internet for

when looking up the plot summary.

The Man on the Mountain

Of course when I hike Tuckerman's Ravine, I go there prepared.

Even if I don't ski, I strategically eat to hike fast.

I also carry a camera in order to capture tree lines up the mountain.

Scaling the bowl is tough, its terrain. The slope is dangerous.

The trail is clearly marked and I listen to advice, even if

I get to a point where I am by myself. Stopping to sit on a rock

on the way up is deliberate, I need to drink water.

The threat of falling ice or rocks makes one hesitant but I still hike.

The trip down the mountain is as laborious as going up.

You still have to be mindful of rocks and those ice patches.

Even the parking lot can pose an immediate threat.

Me and my uncles see a car we don't recognize and they suggest I wander

over and ask what type of car that is.

I follow instruction. Upon asking, I am told that car is completely
  automatic.

I tell them I have never heard of it.

They ask me where I have been living and I reply "This state."

They then instruct me to yell and ask my uncles if they have heard of it.

So I do and my uncles have heard of it.

Grocery Store Versus Mall

To go to the mall is going to intend to shop.
You may or may not hold a bag.

But a shopping cart in a grocery store makes
an entirely different scene and scenario.

It's an object. It will be used.
You don't invite your best friend grocery shopping

whereas at the mall it can become uncomfortable
to state you cannot afford something.

For the Farm's Sake

A scarecrow is a hindrance to a predator.
A scarecrow is markedly placed on private property.

Its usefulness is hopefully public information.
We cannot be certain it was that scarecrow

that disgraced its owner with uselessness.
That is falling from grace but with fertile land.

This is not the same Jim Crow law or ordained
grandfather clause. Farming is like heritage.

We cannot imagine the same face on the same
scarecrow while crows perch on its arms.

Colosseum Delivered

The Colosseum is a monument,
still intact, which relates to
all of mankind. A gladiator

knows the difference between
amphitheatre and theatre.
The structure's mission

is to oversee at all costs
in order to overcome history.
Presently, the foundation

has acquired vegetation
as a reluctant approach to
either approval or forgiveness.

This place was used for real
violence, not mock violence.
Destruction has occurred

intentionally for not upholding
its façade is again damaged
which is not considered sinful.

Bald Eagle Territory

A bald eagle can only soar for so long.
One soared over a zoo in America.
It flew above the entrance, ignoring
the fences, and therefore it's overhead.

If it landed would it become captive

in captivity? Lacking the sufficient

acknowledgement, this bird can

unimaginably become extinct.

To Play Hookey

is to skip school.

But when you skip

school, you learn

nothing. You learn

only the truth.

Follow the Yellow Brick Road, Continued

The wizard in this piece fits nowhere.
The Village of Chittenango luckily borders
Sylvan Beach, which is on Oneida Lake.

There is a two-lane highway to get one
to the nearest hamlet, McConnellsville.
Home of Harden Furniture Showroom.

There is a Harden factory across the street
from the showroom parking lot.
Below ground, there is a tunnel

the factory workmen can walk through,
maybe during lunch. This hamlet is so small
it is considered part of Vienna, near Rome,

which are towns running along Route
13. Neither Rome nor Vienna is the capital
of New York, but sound like they could be.

Here, buying furniture anywhere
but at Harden is forbidden. If delivery arrives
not in a red Harden truck, they'll know.

The Weight of the Hook

To those who do it, fly fishing runs
on rule of thumb. To others,
this activity might go unnoticed.
But casting is so strategic. This pastime
represents the weight of the hook.

A Movie about Brazil That Shows Us What We Do Not Understand

I love the movie *City of God.*
The chicken scenes create
unusual cinematography.

The cachaça appears while
we see men slaughtering
a chicken. Because we are

American and do not know
what we are seeing, we are slow
to call out "slum" or "poverty."

The African Refugee in Vermont Learns about Student Loans

What is relocation?

Is it Burlington, VT,

where white university students

witness refugees for the first time?

In order to graduate from this place

you need to endure exit counseling

and set up your payment plan.

I don't think the harsh winter

is a shock, but all the whiteness may be.

Vermonters can't escape the difference.

Well, for everyone, there's good news:

Vermont student loan servicing

equips students with a grace period

in order to avoid interest

on federal loans.

How Dangerous is a Tear?

When hiding

in a tree?

Is it the actual

telling of life

versus death?

It is definitely

not like jumping

and knowing

you have to land

the fall.

Different Suns

Sunrise is different
than sunset. Overall,

sunrise reflects
what could come

without proof.
And sunset

surpasses only
that already seen.

Tom Versus Huck

The character foil related
to Tom Sawyer and Huck

or Huckleberry Finn holds
true given their upbringing.

Their painting of a fence
is not their character flaw.

Do we consider them brothers?
Some sort of brotherhood bond exists.

The Smithsonian has not
yet divulged Tom as orphan.

Notarize This

A notorious drug dealer
is like a public notary.

Many people who want
to volunteer need to pass

a criminal background check,
then get a document notarized

by an official, who is actually
not obliged to help you.

The Bandit Trio

That group
of bandits

who refer
to each other

as the trio,
they know how

to civilize
crowds via

thought control
via passivity.

Group Home America

What is a group home girl?
A civilian American, located

in adolescent public housing
which analyzes her discourse.

The times she says "snitch"
to refer to those who oppose

other girls is too controlling.
Possibly, compromising for her.

Nancy Drew Helps Youth

I read all Nancy Drew books.
Why? Because they were all
unique but consistent. Simply,
the hardback was buyable.

Ordering KFC

Ordering KFC is truly different,
especially if you are not used to fast food.

We ordered the meal while on vacation
in Sea Island, GA. The dinner was served

buffet style and did not end with dessert.
We then, traditionally, played a round

of hearts. Nobody could shoot the moon,
not because cocktails were served as usual.

What is Free Speech?

Is it an opinion
about pepper spray?

Or a CEO's
authorization of it?

Hollywood Roll Call

The Hollywood sign is a manmade symbol.

But unfortunately it is the victim to vandalism.

It also has supporters that are non-profit.

They support its integrity and longevity.

In an industry that can become scary,

the sign surfaces as a call for actresses.

Driving

In the early months of summer
You can see pollen in the air
While driving near Amsterdam,
NY. This highway is a two-lane
highway going to and from
some destination.

Nursing Home Reputation

The nursing home is across the street
from a quarry. The view from the facility

is scenic: there are birdfeeders to watch
and the landscaping is well maintained.

The staff are instructed to be cordial
because The Nottingham is considered

nice for elders to reside; people visit there.
Visiting hours are not restricted, nor is seating.

Modern-Day Lie

The Indian reservation nowadays is actually
still territorial. They maintain themselves

without outside influence. For instance,
the reservation-owned gas station in central

NY has no commercial interest in another
reservation, or, per se, stealing a tomahawk.

Apparently, alcoholism rates are high
and autonomy is a known concept.

But they do not outcry over state lines.
If only John Smith and Pocahontas married.

A Good Book

The Outsiders was a good book.
The story between the lines

captures the theory behind
socioeconomic status, mainly

adolescents coming to know
themselves in a world which

is allegedly black and white,
to them, and they can't get help.

Democracy

The Bolshevik Times could have been a newspaper name.
Now and in historical times, that name represents separation

of Marxism and Communism. To choose a side, if given
a chance or an option, would be too risky. We know societal

facts and that Communism and all its counterparts are not
capitalism, what we live in, in America. A newspaper

is still in print and was printing back then during
the war. Its use is to support and uphold democracy.

Is a newspaper useless and fake money, like counterfeit?
No, it's a material that secures the industry of modernity.

Bottom Line

"Bottom line" is a common
statement to some. Its intent,

when used appropriately,
is to insert authority.

So, when we hear
it used inappropriately

we wonder how that person
who used it came to be.

Maybe you or they decided
to teach a lesson illegally.

It's just that language carries
weight and we learn

to remember and to not forget
because in the end we heard it.

The Laundromat

A laundromat is not just for the evicted,
it's for those who need it.

I once lived in Spanish Harlem
and that's where I did laundry.

It's not used to expose someone
because it's difficult to get quarters.

Singing on Purpose

Would my dad prefer if I was alto or soprano in seventh grade? Well, my opinion is that soprano is more feminine and therefore more acceptable. The time came to find out. I was told that I am alto. I was shocked. But I also understood that everyone heard the decision. I am an alto. But I am not the teacher who decides, nor can I change my singing voice to a higher pitch on purpose.

The Centennial

Preparation for the centennial was publicly obligatory in Rome.
That year, though the Pope still held public mass on Christmas.

The Vatican City must have overseen the process. At the end
of 1999 the Sistine Chapel was under restoration, to prepare.

Therefore, was not accepting visitors. Apparently all doors
and outside handles were being renovated. I cannot remember

if Florence underwent the same work. Tourists apparently
were not deterred because Rome in general is worth seeing.

Saturday Afternoon

To draw attention to something else,
there are altar boys and girls, persons.

An altar person's personal duty is not
just the bread and wine of Christ.

You must be prepared for five p.m. mass
on a Saturday. That mass time is a conscious

decision on behalf of the altar person. Early
arrival is observed, not looked down upon.

Private Credentialing

In the healthcare industry, private credentialing is an unknown reality.

This concept reflects the act of a practitioner who wants someone

That they professionally know to attach their private practice with the

Local community health practice where they also work. The stigma attached

Involves misuse of personnel and billing practices, while still prescribing.

Canada Neighbors the U.S.

Canada is not like *Jeopardy* in America, that game show on national TV.

Canada is a part of the North American continent, unlike Mexico.

As far as the internet is concerned, their Father's Day is not a public
holiday.

Atomic Bomb

Apparently the light of the atomic bomb was brighter than the sun.
Was the idea behind the creation of the bomb included in that unique
Phrase "on the bright side?" We don't think so, because the bomb
Was and is so controversial that the modernization of weapons may
Or may not include nuclear warfare. Today, we look for answers.

Apartheid Forgotten

Apartheid
is like a ghost
from the past.

We still
are needing
to decipher

its existence
and monitor
its presence.

Earthquake Beware

Imagine living
on a fault line.

Before
the devastation

strikes,
is there

a constant
scenario

of "what if?"
Unknown victims

are not
instructed

to run. Nor
are relatives

told the
actual severity.

Until after
the mass

has fallen
and we awaken.

A native of Syracuse, New York, Elizabeth Carmer earned bachelor's degrees in both Art History and Spanish from the University of Vermont, where she spent time abroad honing her language skills and researching for her future writing. After graduating, Carmer began a career in public health, working as an administrative assistant at a community health center in New Hampshire. Having volunteered internationally and locally for community and women's health organizations, including a domestic violence office and Planned Parenthood, as well as a political campaign, Carmer uses her love of writing to harness in her poems a keen eye for culture, politics, place, and the world around her. Her poems are reflective and autobiographical in nature, and outward-facing in thematic scope.

Currently, Carmer spends her time out of work writing and engaging her passion for photography. *Halfway Friends for Decades* is her first work. Her website is elizabethcarmer.com.

*****

Made in the USA
Lexington, KY
15 September 2019